I WONDER Why

Penguins
Can't Fly

and other questions
about polar lands

Pat Jacobs

KINGFISHER

KINGFISHER

First published in 2011 by Kingfisher
an imprint of Macmillan Children's Books
a division of Macmillan Publishers Limited
20 New Wharf Road, London N1 9RR
Basingstoke and Oxford
Associated companies throughout the world
www.panmacmillan.com

Consultant: David Burnie

ISBN: 978-0-7534-3247-1

9 8 7 6 5 4 3 2 1
SPL/1010/WKT/UNTD/140MA

A CIP catalogue record for this book is available from
the British Library.

Printed in China

Illustrations: Martin Camm 6–7, 9bl, 14–15, 16–17, 18–19,
20–21, 22–23, 24–25, 26–27, 30–31; Phil Jacobs 4–5, 8–9,
10–11, 28bl, 29br, 30br, 31br; all cartoons: Peter Wilks
(Plum Pudding).

CONTENTS

4 Where are the poles?

4 Why is Antarctica the highest and
lowest continent?

5 Why are there four poles?

5 How could north become south?

6 Can deserts be snowy?

6 Were the poles always frozen?

7 How cold are the poles?

7 Why is the Antarctic colder than
the Arctic?

8 How are icebergs formed?

8 How thick is polar ice?

9 What is permafrost?

10 What lights up the sky?

10 What is diamond dust?

11 Which dogs are found at the poles?

12 Does anyone live in the Antarctic?

12 Who first came to the poles?

13 Do people still build igloos?

14 Are there any polar plants?

14 How do plants survive the cold?

15 Which tree grows in the 'treeless' tundra?

16 How do animals survive the Arctic winter?

16 Why aren't polar bears white?

17 Which creatures change colour?

18 Which animal bullies bigger beasts?

19 How do musk-oxen protect their young?

20 Who puts puffins in danger?

21 Which bird migrates from pole to pole?

21 Are there pirates at the poles?

22 Why can't penguins fly?

23 Why don't polar bears eat penguins?

23 Why don't penguins' eggs freeze?

24 Which seal is a champion diver?

25 Where would you find a 'bloodless' fish?

25 Who is called the 'unicorn of the sea'?

26 Which greedy guest eats four tonnes a day?

26 Why are polar seas so lively?

27 What are krill?

28 What does Antarctica tell us about space?

28 Why is Antarctica a meteorite hot spot?

29 Why is the ice like a time machine?

30 Who pollutes the poles?

30 What is the ozone hole?

31 What if all the polar ice melted?

31 Who lives where?

32 Index

Where are the poles?

The North Pole lies at the centre of the Arctic Circle. At the North Pole, wherever you turn, you will be heading south. The South Pole is at the opposite end of the Earth, in the middle of the Antarctic Circle on the continent of Antarctica.

Antarctic Circle

geographic South Pole

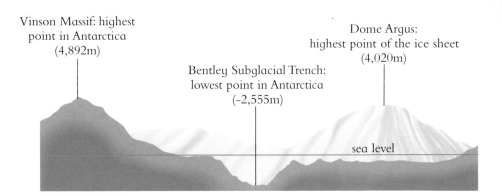

Vinson Massif: highest point in Antarctica (4,892m)

Bentley Subglacial Trench: lowest point in Antarctica (-2,555m)

Dome Argus: highest point of the ice sheet (4,020m)

sea level

Why is Antarctica the highest and lowest continent?

The thick ice sheet makes Antarctica the world's highest continent, with an average height of 2,400 metres. At 2,555 metres below sea level, the Bentley Subglacial Trench in West Antarctica is the lowest place on Earth that is not under water.

At the poles, the sun rises and sets only once a year, so a day lasts for 12 months. Because the Earth is tilted, one pole faces the sun for six months while the other is dark, then the opposite pole has six months of daylight.

Good night!

geographic North Pole

Arctic Circle

Why are there four poles?

The Earth is a giant magnet, which is why a compass points to the North Pole. The geographic North and South Poles are fixed points, but because the Earth's magnetic field is always changing, the magnetic North and South Poles move every day.

magnetic North Pole

How could north become south?

Every so often, the Earth's magnetic field reverses, so a compass that pointed north would point south. This last occurred more than 780,000 years ago and scientists think it is due to happen again.

North Pole

Can deserts be snowy?

Very cold air cannot hold much water, so it rarely snows at the poles. Parts of the Arctic are as dry as the Sahara and Antarctica is the driest continent on Earth – making it the world's biggest desert.

a camel in the Sahara – the world's largest hot desert

Were the poles always frozen?

About 100–65 million years ago, the climate was warmer than it is today and the polar ice caps did not exist. Forests reached as far as the South Pole and were home to dinosaurs such as *Antarctopelta* (left).

Antarctica is the world's windiest place. The winds that blow around the coast can reach speeds of about 300 kilometres an hour.

a polar bear in the Arctic – the world's second largest cold desert

How cold are the poles?

In Antarctica, in 1983, a temperature of -89.2°C was recorded, which is cold enough to freeze the mercury in a thermometer. The winter temperature at the North Pole averages -34°C. That is 15°C colder than your freezer.

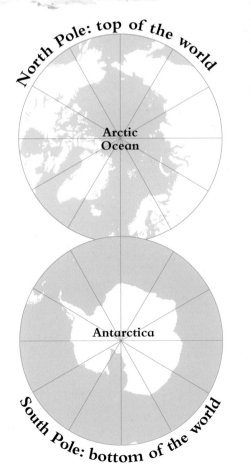

North Pole: top of the world

Arctic Ocean

Antarctica

South Pole: bottom of the world

Why is the Antarctic colder than the Arctic?

Antarctica is a continent surrounded by the sea, while the Arctic is an ocean surrounded by land. Water stays warmer than land during winter, so on average the Antarctic is about 17°C colder than the Arctic.

How are icebergs formed?

Icebergs are huge blocks of freshwater ice that break off from glaciers or from the ice shelf and float out to sea. The largest known iceberg was bigger than the island of Jamaica and the tallest was the height of a 55-storey building.

How thick is polar ice?

Sea ice in the Arctic is about three metres thick during the winter. The thickest ice is found in the Bentley Subglacial Trench, the lowest point in Antarctica. Here the ice measures 4,776 metres – that is almost six times the height of the Burj Khalifa in Dubai.

At 828 metres, the Burj Khalifa building in Dubai, in the Middle East, is the tallest in the world.

Ice flows slowly from the centre of Antarctica to the coast. An iceberg floating in the sea today could contain snow that fell at the South Pole during the time of the Neanderthals, early humans who lived about 100,000 years ago.

Only one-eighth of an iceberg can be seen. The rest is hidden below the water.

Small icebergs are called 'growlers', because they often make a growling noise as trapped air escapes from the ice.

What is permafrost?

Permafrost is ground that is frozen all year round. In 2007, a perfectly preserved baby mammoth, thought to have died 10,000 years ago, was unearthed from the permafrost in Siberia, Russia.

What lights up the sky?

The solar wind carries electrically charged particles from the sun towards Earth. Some particles enter our atmosphere above the magnetic poles and collide with Earth's gases, creating a fantastic light show called the northern or southern lights.

What is diamond dust?

When the air temperature is very low, water vapour in the atmosphere freezes to form tiny ice crystals. These catch the sun and sparkle like a sprinkling of diamonds in the sky.

A whiteout occurs when low white clouds cover the sky and the snow and sky merge into one. People say it is like being trapped inside a huge white ball.

Which dogs are found at the poles?

A Brocken spectre is a large, ghostly figure with a rainbow halo. It is actually a person's shadow cast by a low sun onto distant fog.

Sun dogs are bright flares that appear on either side of the sun when ice crystals in the sky reflect the sunlight. Moon dogs are sometimes seen, too, when the moon is very bright.

Does anyone live in the Antarctic?

No one lives there permanently, but Antarctica is visited by about 4,000 scientists during the summer. Only about 1,000 stay to brave the cold, dark winter though.

Who first came to the poles?

American explorers Frederick Cook and Robert Peary both claimed to have reached the North Pole first – Cook in 1908 and Peary in 1909. Roald Amundsen led the first expedition to the South Pole, arriving in December 1911.

Early polar explorers used huskies to haul their sleds, but now dogs are banned from Antarctica to protect the wildlife.

Researchers at Antarctica's Concordia Station, studying the effects of living in space, are trying to find out if wearing bedsocks at night would help astronauts to sleep.

Do people still build igloos?

The word 'iglu' means house in the Inuit language. So people in the Arctic do live in 'iglus', but igloos made of snow are now built only as temporary shelters during hunting trips.

Traditional explorers' rations included pemmican (dried meat and fat) and sledging biscuits. In 1999, a biscuit from Scott's 1910 expedition was sold for £3,900.

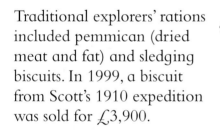

broken biscuit
£3,900

H P

Norwegian Roald Amundsen reached the South Pole one month before Britain's Captain Robert Falcon Scott.

Are there any polar plants?

The poles are covered in ice all year round but plants grow in less cold areas, called the tundra. For a few weeks in mid-summer, the Arctic tundra is carpeted in colour as plants that have spent the winter beneath the snow burst into flower.

The tundra's flowers attract lots of insects, so birds flock there in summer to raise their families and make the most of the insect feast.

How do plants survive the cold?

Tundra plants huddle close to the ground in tight clumps and often have hairy leaves and stems to protect them from the cold. Cup-shaped flowers follow the sun as it moves across the sky.

A snowy owl catches a lemming for its chicks.

Which tree grows in the 'treeless' tundra?

The word 'tundra' comes from a Finnish word meaning 'treeless plain', so you would not expect to find any trees there. Yet a willow, just 20 centimetres tall, has adapted to the cold, windy climate and provides food for caribou, musk-oxen, Arctic hares and lemmings.

Most owls are active only when it is dark, but snowy owls hunt in daylight, too – otherwise they would starve during the Arctic summer, when the sun never sets.

Permafrost stops melting snow sinking into the ground, so it forms pools that are perfect nurseries for mosquito larvae (young). Sometimes the mosquito swarms are so large, they turn the sky grey.

Arctic willow

In summer, animals such as snowy owls and caribou take advantage of the plentiful food to raise their young and fatten up for the winter.

caribou

15

How do animals survive the Arctic winter?

In winter, temperatures in the Arctic drop to -50°C, so polar animals grow a thick winter coat to keep them warm. The Arctic fox even has fur on the bottom of its feet and uses its bushy tail as a blanket.

Beneath its thick coat, the polar bear has black skin, which absorbs heat from the sun and keeps the bear warm.

The Arctic fox can hear small animals moving in their underground burrows. It pounces to break through the snow, then grabs its prey.

Why aren't polar bears white?

If you plucked a few hairs from a polar bear, you would find they are colourless. Like snow and ice, they are translucent – light passes through them, but they look white to us.

Collared lemmings are a favourite food for Arctic predators. A large family of Arctic foxes can eat up to 4,000 before the young leave the den.

Which creatures change colour?

Arctic wolves, foxes and ermines turn white in winter so they can creep up on their prey without being seen. Arctic hares and collared lemmings grow white fur, too, so predators find them hard to spot in the snow.

The Arctic ground squirrel hibernates from September to April to escape the winter cold. Its body temperature drops to -3°C during its seven-month sleep.

Which animal bullies bigger beasts?

The wolverine (below) is a fast and fierce hunter, armed with strong jaws and sharp claws. Arctic hares, squirrels and birds are easy prey, but this dog-sized predator also steals kills from bears and cougars, and sometimes attacks much larger animals, such as caribou.

A wolverine steals food from a grizzly bear.

In late summer, caribou stamp their feet, shake their heads and run about wildly. They are trying to escape the warble flies that lay their eggs in the caribou's fur.

18

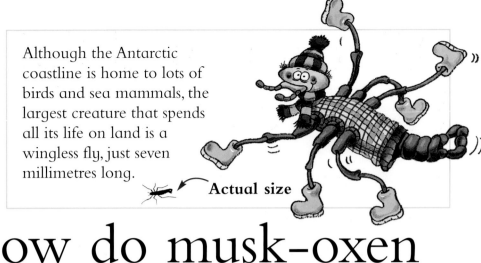

Although the Antarctic coastline is home to lots of birds and sea mammals, the largest creature that spends all its life on land is a wingless fly, just seven millimetres long.

Actual size

How do musk-oxen protect their young?

Adult musk-oxen have sharp horns that can kill or injure the Arctic wolves that prey on the herd. When predators are nearby, the adults form a circle around the young, creating a spiky barricade with their horns.

Musk-oxen have hardly changed since prehistoric times, when they lived alongside woolly mammoths and sabre-toothed tigers.

Who puts puffins in danger?

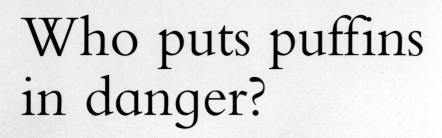

The puffin's natural predators include gulls, skuas, foxes, sharks and killer whales, but humans are the greatest threat to their survival. Puffins feed on fish and other sea creatures, so they are endangered by overfishing and oil spills. In some places, people still eat puffins and their eggs.

Puffins have backward-pointing spines in their tongues and the tops of their mouths to hold on to their fishy catch. One puffin was seen with more than 60 fish in its beak.

A skua chases a kelp gull.

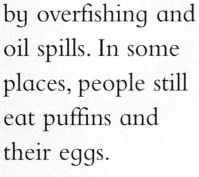

The wandering albatross is a superb flier with the widest wingspan of any bird, but it is very clumsy on land. It often turns somersaults as it crash lands, and regularly trips over its own feet.

Which bird migrates from pole to pole?

The Arctic tern breeds on the tundra, then flies to the Antarctic as winter approaches. It makes the longest migration of any bird, travelling more than 35,000 kilometres each year.

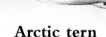

Arctic tern

A skua attacks a penguin colony.

Although they have webbed feet, it seems that Arctic terns do not like water. They swoop down to catch fish, but do their best to avoid getting wet.

Are there pirates at the poles?

Skuas are nicknamed 'pirates' because they steal food from other birds in mid-air. They target penguin colonies, too, often working in pairs. While one distracts the penguin, the other steals its egg or chick.

King penguins
dive down
300 metres in
search of fish
and squid.

Why can't penguins fly?

Most birds have lightweight skeletons, but penguins have heavy, solid bones and a thick layer of fat to keep them warm. They would need huge wings to lift themselves into the air. Instead, their wings have turned into stiff little flippers, which power their streamlined bodies through the water.

penguin wing

gull wing

Why don't polar bears eat penguins?

A polar bear would have to swim a long way to eat a penguin because they live at opposite ends of the Earth. Polar bears live in the Arctic and penguins are found only south of the equator.

At 1.7 metres tall, a penguin that waddled the Earth around 40 million years ago could easily have pecked a man in the eye. Fossils of this Antarctic giant were found on Seymour Island.

Why don't penguins' eggs freeze?

An emperor penguin's egg would freeze in minutes if it were left on the ice, so the penguins balance their eggs on their feet and keep them warm inside a brood pouch. This is a flap of featherless skin that wraps around the egg.

Which seal is a champion diver?

Weddell seals dive down to 700 metres in search of fish and squid, and can stay underwater for more than an hour. Their strong teeth help to chew breathing holes in the ice and they sometimes blow air into cracks in the ice to startle fish – which then swim right into the seals' mouths.

southernmost seal

Weddell seals live in the Antarctic, further south than any other seal.

Polar fish have antifreeze in their blood to stop them freezing solid. This fish antifreeze is sometimes used to stop ice crystals forming in ice cream.

Where would you find a 'bloodless' fish?

The crocodile icefish that lives in the sea around Antarctica has no red blood cells, so its blood is clear, just like water. The fish gets its name from its long snout, which is packed with white teeth.

Who is called the 'unicorn of the sea'?

The male narwhal's unicorn-like tusk is actually an overgrown tooth. When the whale is one year old, one of his two top teeth grows through his lip. A ten-year-old narwhal's tusk can be three metres in length.

As walruses warm up in the sun, blood flows to the surface of their skin and they turn from muddy brown to pink.

Which greedy guest eats four tonnes a day?

The blue whale is the biggest creature ever to have lived, yet it feeds on some of the smallest animals. Blue whales eat krill, swallowing more than four million each day during the summer months when they come to feed in the polar waters.

Why are polar seas so lively?

The oceans around the poles are teeming with life. Cold water absorbs more oxygen and currents carry nutrients to the surface, where they feed the phytoplankton – microscopic plants eaten by krill, which are an important food for many sea creatures.

sea squirt

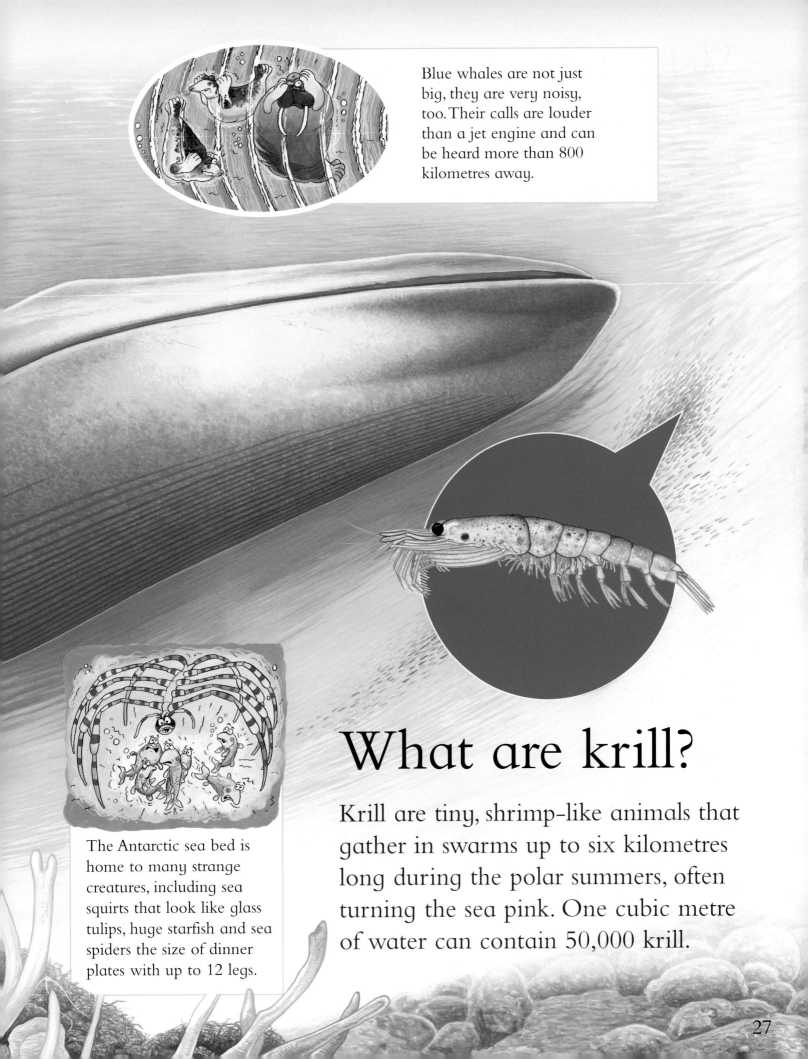

Blue whales are not just big, they are very noisy, too. Their calls are louder than a jet engine and can be heard more than 800 kilometres away.

What are krill?

Krill are tiny, shrimp-like animals that gather in swarms up to six kilometres long during the polar summers, often turning the sea pink. One cubic metre of water can contain 50,000 krill.

The Antarctic sea bed is home to many strange creatures, including sea squirts that look like glass tulips, huge starfish and sea spiders the size of dinner plates with up to 12 legs.

What does Antarctica tell us about space?

The only place colder than Antarctica is outer space, so it is the best place on Earth to test the space robots of the future. Underwater vehicle *Endurance* has been studying Lake Bonney, but one day it might explore the ocean that scientists believe lies beneath the icy crust of Europa, one of Jupiter's largest moons.

Why is Antarctica a meteorite hot spot?

There is nowhere better to search for meteorites because they are so easy to see on the Antarctic ice sheet. *Nomad* is a robotic meteorite hunter that can tell the difference between a meteorite and a normal rock. Some of the meteorites it found had come from Mars.

Scientists have found large amounts of cosmic dust in Antarctic ice cores. They think it fell to Earth when a giant space rock exploded above the continent about 480,000 years ago.

Why is the ice like a time machine?

Each layer of snow contains clues to what is happening in the world. By drilling out cores from the polar ice, scientists can unlock the past and learn about volcanic eruptions, forest fires, dust storms and temperature changes that occurred up to 750,000 years ago.

As the Antarctic is dark both day and night during winter, and the dry air is crystal clear, it is the best place in the world to view the stars.

Ice cores are long cylinders of compacted snow. They contain ash, dust, chemicals, radioactive substances and even material from outer space.

Who pollutes the poles?

Sadly, human activities sometimes produce chemicals and oil spills that pollute our world. Winds and ocean currents may carry these to the poles, where they can harm the creatures that live there.

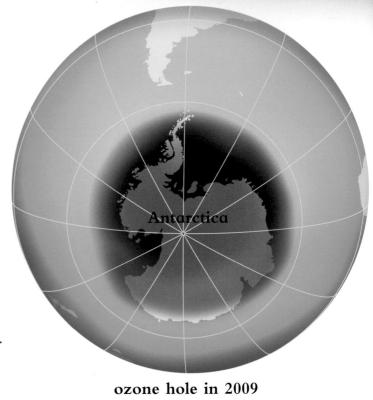

3 When polar bears eat the seals, poisons build up in their bodies.

1 Plankton absorb pollutants and are eaten by fish.

What is the ozone hole?

Ozone is a gas in our upper atmosphere that protects us from harmful ultraviolet rays from the sun. Man-made chemicals can destroy ozone and, each spring, the ozone layer above Antarctica has been getting thinner. A smaller ozone hole has recently appeared over the Arctic, too.

Antarctica

ozone hole in 2009

high ozone   low ozone

What if all the polar ice melted?

If the polar ice caps melted, the sea would rise by about 60 metres and many low-lying countries would be flooded – but it would take thousands of years for this to happen.

2 Seals eat the fish and the harmful chemicals are stored in their fat.

Who lives where?

These lists are a guide to the natural habitat(s) of the animals shown in this book.

Arctic
Arctic fox
Arctic ground squirrel
Arctic hare
Arctic wolf
caribou (also called reindeer)
collared lemming
ermine (also called stoat)
grizzly bear
musk-ox
narwhal
polar bear
puffin
snowy owl
walrus
wolverine

Antarctic
crocodile icefish
kelp gull
penguin
wandering albatross
Weddell seal

Arctic and Antarctic
Arctic tern
blue whale
krill
skua

Index

A

albatrosses 20, 31
Amundsen, Roald 12, 13
Antarctic Circle 4, 6
Arctic Circle 4, 5, 6
Arctic foxes 16, 17, 20, 31
Arctic hares 15, 17, 18, 31
Arctic terns 21, 31

B

Bentley Subglacial Trench 4, 8
birds 14, 18, 20, 21
biscuits, sledging 13
blue whales 26, 27, 31
Brocken spectres 11

C

caribou 15, 18, 31
compasses 4
Cook, Frederick 12
crocodile icefish 25, 31

D

daylight 4, 15
deserts 6
diamond dust 10
dinosaurs 6
dogs 12

E

eggs 18, 20, 21, 23
ermines 17, 31

F

fish 20, 24, 25, 30, 31
flies 18, 19

G

geographic poles 5
grizzly bears 18, 19, 31
ground squirrels 17, 18, 31
growlers 9

H

hibernation 17

I

ice 8, 10, 14, 24, 29
ice cores 29
icebergs 8, 9
igloos 13
insects 14, 15, 19

K

krill 26, 27, 31

L

lemmings 15, 17, 31

M

magnetic poles 5, 10
mammoths 9, 19
meteorites 28
migration 21
moon dogs 11
mosquitos 15
musk-oxen 15, 19, 31

N

narwhals 25, 31
North Pole 4, 5, 7, 12
northern lights 10

O

ozone hole 30

P

Peary, Robert 12
pemmican 13
penguins 21, 22, 23, 31
permafrost 9, 15
plankton 26, 30
plants 14, 15
polar bears 7, 16, 23, 30, 31
pollution 30
puffins 20, 31

R

reindeer 31
robots 28

S

Scott, Captain 13
sea spiders 27
sea squirts 27
seals 24, 31
skuas 20, 21, 31
snowy owls 15, 31
solar wind 10
South Pole 4, 5, 7, 12
southern lights 10
space 28, 29
starfish 27
stoats 31
sun dogs 11

T

temperature 7, 10, 16
trees 15
tundra 14, 15

W

walruses 25, 31
whales 20, 25, 26, 27, 31
whiteouts 11
willow 15
wind 7, 15, 30
  see also solar wind
wolverines 18, 31
wolves, Arctic 17, 19, 31